AMANDA MURPHY'S

FREE-MOTION QUILTING

WORKBOOK

20 ALLOVER DESIGNS TO PRACTICE & LEARN
STEP-BY-STEP INSTRUCTIONS

By Amanda Murphy

C&T PUBLISHING
Another Maker Inspired!

Publisher: Amy Barrett-Daffin

Creative Director: Gailen Runge

Senior Editor: Roxane Cerda

Cover/Book Designer: April Mostek

Production Coordinator: Tim Manibusan

Illustrator: Amanda Murphy

Photography Coordinator: Rachel Ackley

Front cover photography by Amanda Murphy

Author photography by BERNINA of America.

Published by C&T Publishing, Inc., P.O. Box 1456, Lafayette, CA 94549

DEDICATION

*For my students,
who give me all my best ideas!*

ACKNOWLEDGMENTS

Special thanks to the great people at C&T Publishing who made this book possible, including, but not limited to, Todd Hensley, Amy Barrett-Daffin, Gailen Runge, April Mostek, Betsy LaHonta, and Tim Manibusan. Last but not least, to my awesome editor and amazing friend Roxane Cerda, who always knows how to elicit my best ideas. In this case, to draw a book, rather than write one!

CONTENTS

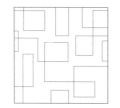

INTRODUCTION

My favorite quilts feature a combination of free-motion motifs and rulerwork. Rulerwork adds structure while free-motion designs add an organic feel and dynamic movement, making the combination shine all the more brightly! I don't like repetition, so I typically use multiple free-motion patterns in a quilt or combine elements from some of my favorites to create an entirely new design.

However, I clearly remember that when I started quilting, I found anything beyond loops or a meander massively intimidating: And I draw for a living! So, the question became how can I create a book that teaches people to explore quilt patterns beyond a basic meander?

ADDING NEW DESIGNS TO YOUR REPERTOIRE

Whether you are completely new to quilting, have mastered a few basic designs, or consider yourself an experienced quilter who would like to expand your pattern repertoire, this book can help you improve your skills by introducing you to common quilting motifs and shapes, and allowing you space to practice drawing them. I've chosen to show some of my favorite open (meaning that I don't quilt back over my previously-quilted lines) free-motion quilting patterns. These are the quickest types of patterns to quilt and they can be combined in an infinite number of ways.

Adding new quilt designs to your arsenal can seem challenging, but when you work through it step by step, it's a snap. In this workbook, you'll find 20 allover designs that range from simple to more complicated, so it will be easy to find one to compliment your quilt top. By tracing, then partially drawing, and finally drawing the patterns independently, you'll learn new shapes and how to combine them.

DO MY SHAPES NEED TO LOOK EXACTLY LIKE YOURS?

Definitely not! Quilting is like handwriting, and because of that, it is difficult to imitate someone's quilting exactly. It would be like forging a signature. Everyone's quilting will look a little different, and guess what? In hundreds of years, people looking at our quilts (and even our mistakes) will know a computer didn't do all the work and they will be more valued because of it!

My hope is that you can use this book as a launch pad to explore more patterns and ideas on your own.

HOW TO USE THIS BOOK

There are 20 designs in this book, and each design spans 4 pages.

On the first page, I'll walk you through how I drew the design, step by step. Begin at the point of the design indicated by a small magenta circle. Trace along the drawn line until you hit the edge of the quilting area. Travel along that edge to continue.

A simple traveling line.

START

↑ Continue quilting.

Sometimes, when you reach the edge of the quilting area, you might notice a blank space without quilting that you missed. Travel back along the edge and fill the space with partial shapes that you are already using in this design.

Going back and filling in areas along the edges with similar shapes.

Sometimes, the traveling can be quite complex, particularly when you get to the top of a quilted area. You might have to quilt numerous partial motifs, but no worries! There are many ways to fill these areas and, as long as you stick to shapes you are already using, there is no right or wrong way to proceed!

Continue tracing the design, traveling along the edge of the illustration as necessary, to fill the page.

On the second page, trace my drawing to get started. Remember, you'll need to backtrack from time to time and add in partial motifs to fill in the inevitable open spaces along the edges of your quilted area!

On the third page, I just give you a hint of what's to come and you fill in the rest.

The fourth page is all you. Remember, your designs don't have to look exactly like mine!

> *Tip* **DRAW using your whole arm, rather than just your wrist. It will make the drawn line smoother and put less strain on your body!**

A more complex fill. Note that the travel lines along the edge, shown in magenta, are separated here for clarity. They would be on top of each other on an actual quilt.

Tip **If in doubt of how to get to another part of the quilting area, ECHO!**

DO I STILL HAVE TO PRACTICE QUILTING ON A MACHINE?

Unfortunately, yes. This book will teach your head how to create the designs, but teaching your hands takes time and repetition. If you become frustrated with this please remember that you would not expect someone to play a concert the first time they sat down at a piano! I recommend practicing quilting 15–20 minutes per day, 3–4 times a week. In just three months you'll have a lot more control.

Tip **Just as you did when you were drawing, QUILT use your entire arms, rather than just your wrists. It will make the quilted lines smoother and put less strain on your body!**

WHAT IF I FORGET TO QUILT AN AREA IN THE CENTER OF MY QUILTING?

Do not, I repeat, **do not** rip out all your stitching. That would be time from your life you won't get back!

Start at an area adjacent to the open area, on top of a previously drawn/quilted line. Snake into the area, fill it with the same design, and then snake back out, ending on a previously quilted line.

No one will notice unless you tell them, which you won't, because you'll be too busy doing more quilting!

Filling in an area in the center.

Onward, quilting friends!
Time to draw!

AMANDA MURPHY'S FREE-MOTION QUILTING WORKBOOK

START

START

AMANDA MURPHY'S FREE-MOTION QUILTING WORKBOOK

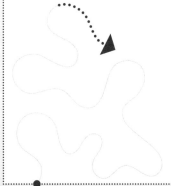

START

START

Note that the travel lines along the edge, shown in magenta, are separated here for clarity.
They would be on top of each other on an actual quilt.

START

START

AMANDA MURPHY'S FREE-MOTION QUILTING WORKBOOK

START

Note that the travel lines along the edge, shown in magenta, are separated here for clarity.
They would be on top of each other on an actual quilt.

START

AMANDA MURPHY'S FREE-MOTION QUILTING WORKBOOK

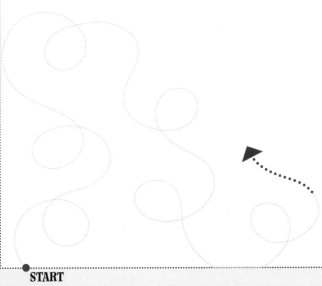

START

START

Note that the travel lines along the edge, shown in magenta, are separated here for clarity.
They would be on top of each other on an actual quilt.

START

AMANDA MURPHY'S FREE-MOTION QUILTING WORKBOOK

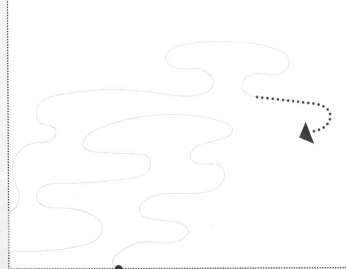

START

START

Note that the travel lines along the edge, shown in magenta, are separated here for clarity.
They would be on top of each other on an actual quilt.

START

AMANDA MURPHY'S FREE-MOTION QUILTING WORKBOOK

START

27

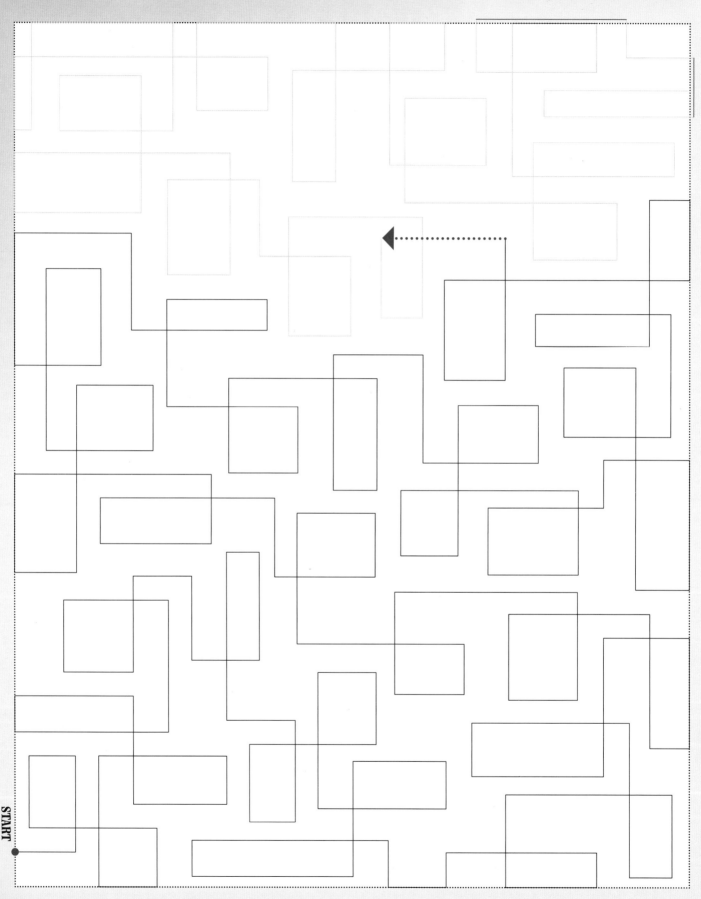

START

Note that the travel lines along the edge, shown in magenta, are separated here for clarity.
They would be on top of each other on an actual quilt.

START

AMANDA MURPHY'S FREE-MOTION QUILTING WORKBOOK

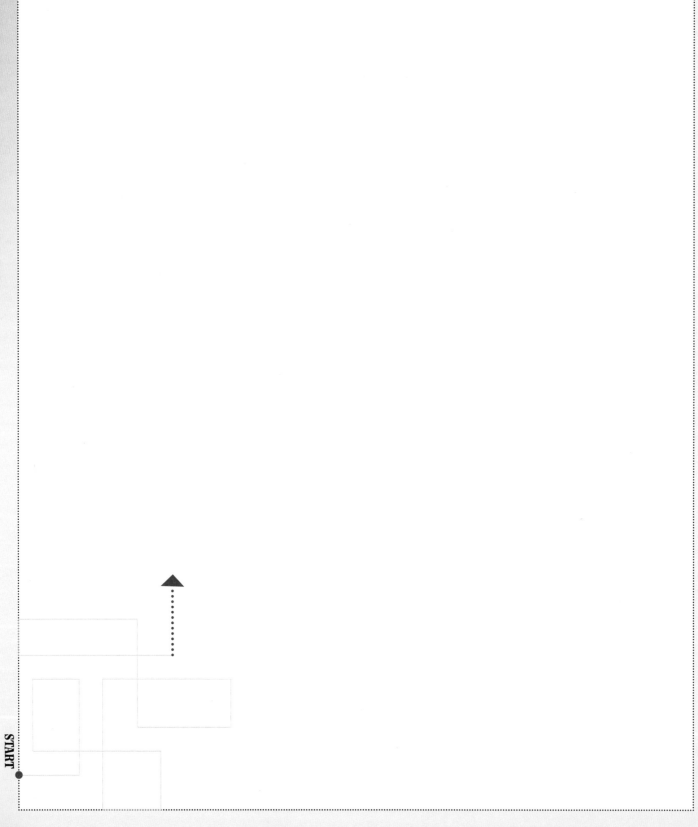

START

AMANDA MURPHY'S FREE-MOTION QUILTING WORKBOOK

START

Note that the travel lines along the edge, shown in magenta, are separated here for clarity.
They would be on top of each other on an actual quilt.

START

34

AMANDA MURPHY'S FREE-MOTION QUILTING WORKBOOK

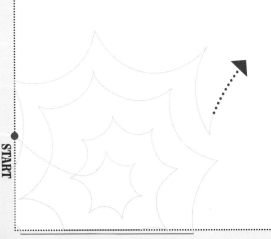

START

AMANDA MURPHY'S FREE-MOTION QUILTING WORKBOOK

START

Note that the travel lines along the edge, shown in magenta, are separated here for clarity.
They would be on top of each other on an actual quilt.

START

AMANDA MURPHY'S FREE-MOTION QUILTING WORKBOOK

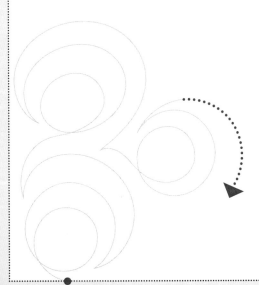

START

OPEN SWIRLS

START

Note that the travel lines along the edge, shown in magenta, are separated here for clarity.
They would be on top of each other on an actual quilt.

START

START

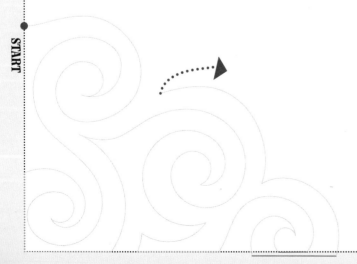

43

START

Note that the travel lines along the edge, shown in magenta, are separated here for clarity.
They would be on top of each other on an actual quilt.

START

AMANDA MURPHY'S FREE-MOTION QUILTING WORKBOOK

START

AMANDA MURPHY'S FREE-MOTION QUILTING WORKBOOK

START

Note that the travel lines along the edge, shown in magenta, are separated here for clarity.
They would be on top of each other on an actual quilt.

START

AMANDA MURPHY'S FREE-MOTION QUILTING WORKBOOK

START

AMANDA MURPHY'S FREE-MOTION QUILTING WORKBOOK

START

Note that the travel lines along the edge, shown in magenta, are separated here for clarity.
They would be on top of each other on an actual quilt.

START

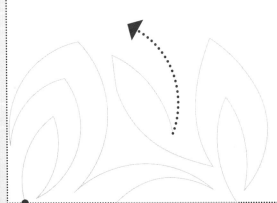

START

AMANDA MURPHY'S FREE-MOTION QUILTING WORKBOOK

START

Note that the travel lines along the edge, shown in magenta, are separated here for clarity.
They would be on top of each other on an actual quilt.

START

AMANDA MURPHY'S FREE-MOTION QUILTING WORKBOOK

START

START

Note that the travel lines along the edge, shown in magenta, are separated here for clarity.
They would be on top of each other on an actual quilt.

START

AMANDA MURPHY'S FREE-MOTION QUILTING WORKBOOK

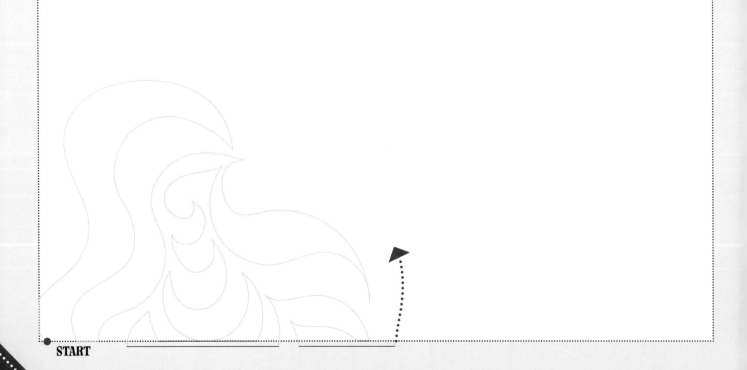

START

START

Note that the travel lines along the edge, shown in magenta, are separated here for clarity.
They would be on top of each other on an actual quilt.

START

AMANDA MURPHY'S FREE-MOTION QUILTING WORKBOOK

START

AMANDA MURPHY'S FREE-MOTION QUILTING WORKBOOK

START

Note that the travel lines along the edge, shown in magenta, are separated here for clarity.
They would be on top of each other on an actual quilt.

START

70

START

AMANDA MURPHY'S FREE-MOTION QUILTING WORKBOOK

START

Note that the travel lines along the edge, shown in magenta, are separated here for clarity.
They would be on top of each other on an actual quilt.

START

START

LOOPED TULIPS WITH LEAVES

START

Note that the travel lines along the edge, shown in magenta, are separated here for clarity.
They would be on top of each other on an actual quilt.

START

AMANDA MURPHY'S FREE-MOTION QUILTING WORKBOOK

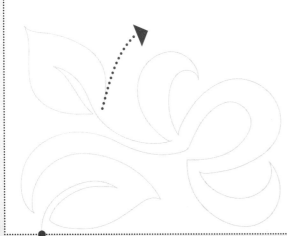

START

START

Note that the travel lines along the edge, shown in magenta, are separated here for clarity.
They would be on top of each other on an actual quilt.

START

AMANDA MURPHY'S FREE-MOTION QUILTING WORKBOOK

START

AMANDA MURPHY'S FREE-MOTION QUILTING WORKBOOK

START

Note that the travel lines along the edge, shown in magenta, are separated here for clarity.
They would be on top of each other on an actual quilt.

START

AMANDA MURPHY'S FREE-MOTION QUILTING WORKBOOK

START

ABOUT THE AUTHOR

Photo by BERNINA International

AMANDA MURPHY is a quilt and fabric designer whose style bridges the modern and traditional. Her quilting is known for its innovative combination of rulerwork, free-motion, and automated designs. She is a BERNINA Expert and Quilting and Longarm Spokesperson, international teacher, pattern designer, and fabric designer for Contempo of Benartex. She designs best-selling quilting rulers and notions for Brewer Sewing, embroidery and quilting collections for OESD, and has authored several books for C&T Publishing including the best-selling *Organic Free-Motion Quilting Idea Book* and *Rulerwork Idea Book*. Amanda also has created a thread line, in conjunction with OESD, called Perfect Quilting Thread. Many know her through her popular live broadcasts on YouTube and Facebook.

Follow Amanda's quilting journey and ask your quilting questions in her Facebook group Quilting with Amanda Murphy.

Quilt with me!

Subscribe to my Youtube Channel
youtube.com/@AmandaMurphyDesign

Join my Facebook Group
Quilting with Amanda Murphy

Visit My Website
amandamurphydesign.com